Business For Profit

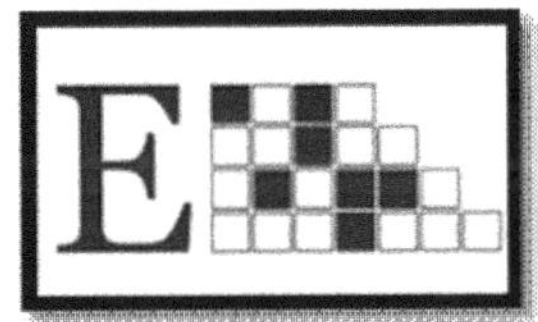

Eurydice Moore, M.A., Ph.D.

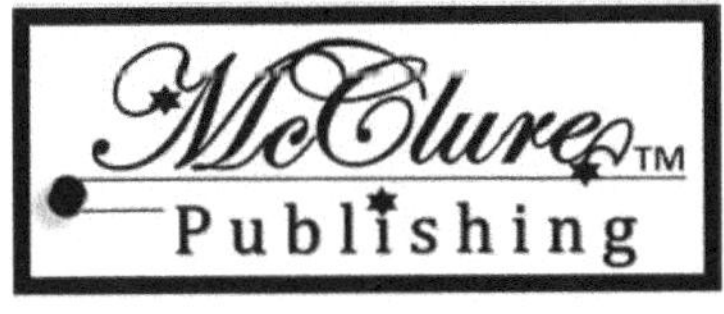

www.mcclurepublishing.com

ISBN 13: 978-0-9989223-2-4

Cover Design and Interior Layout by Kathy McClure
https://www.mcclurepublishing.com

Order additional copies, please contact
books@mcclurepublishing.com
800-659-4908

THIS BOOK PROJECT WAS MADE POSSIBLE THROUGH FUNDING BY:

A partnership with the Chicago Housing Authority (CHA) and Housing Urban Development (HUD)'s Section 3 BUSINESS CONCERN COMPETITIVE GRANT

DISCLAIMER

Dr. Eurydice Moore is not an attorney; therefore, seek legal advice where applicable. The information shared in this book is strictly for educational and informational purpose only. Seek a professional where applicable.

DEDICATION

Rita Nashell McClendon,

I dedicate this book to you for it would not have been possible without you.
I want to thank you for being an armor bearer.

TRIBUTE

Anna White my Maternal Great Grandmother was the first business person that I came in contact. She was an entrepreneur before the phrase was coined in the late 50s.

Anna had the following six incomes:

- Sold sweet potato pies
- Sold snow balls
- Property manager and homeowner
- Sold starch dollies
- Babysat
- Quilt maker and sold quilts

If I equated what she did to today's standards, I would say that she was a realtor, baker, vendor and child care provider. Anna was a very productive woman. She was a polymath individual. I am her descendant and her greatness has trickled to me. I am now walking the path of a polymath individual.

I think about Anna daily, and she is deeply embedded into my heart.

I salute you Anna.

Always and Forever
Eurydice

Table of Contents

Page

Introduction
Business for Profit Questionnaire

Law Depot

INTRODUCTION

The term business is defined in this book, and readers will learn the difference between a domestic and foreign business as well as a Not-for-Profit Corporation and For Profit. The author defines vision statement and mission statement which is required for those seeking to start-up a business. Readers will have the opportunity to assess and compare business versus employment the advantages and disadvantages. The readers will also learn the various business structure options such as Sole Proprietor, Limited Liability Company, partnership, the S and C corporations, and many others. The author will list the up and down sides of businesses, and the character traits needed to launch a business venture. The author will list several common reasons that businesses fail and why.

The reader will learn to do a self-evaluation of credentials, skills, and personality traits in order to determine if a business venture is feasible for oneself. The author will assist the reader in exploring the ten steps in starting a business such as 1) business name, 2) business plan 3) business assistance and trainings, 4) business location, 5) financing the business, 6) legal structure of your business, 7) tax identification number, 8) Dunn & Bradstreet number, 9) registration for state and local taxes, and 10) business licenses and permits, including understanding ones role as a potential employer. The author will conclude the book with ten (10) questions that readers can ask themselves to determine if business is for them. The author will also list resources in which readers can connect to actively pursue the beginning of business start-up, and to receive the technical and supportive services available for those seeking to venture off into business whether part time or full time.

Business For Profit Questionnaire

You want to get into business? First, there are two types of businesses. There are For Profit (FP) and Not-For-Profit (NFP). Which can be domestic (located within the United States) or Foreign (located outside of the United States). Either of them can be domestic or foreign base. Whatever the case, you must first determine if you have the characteristics, skills, and resources to be an entrepreneur, small business person, or president of a NFP. Below are some things to think about before starting a business and to determine if it would be feasible for you to do so:

1. Are your personality characteristics such that you can adapt to and enjoy small business ownership?

   ____
   ____
   ____
   ____

2. What kind of a business do you want?

   ____
   ____
   ____
   ____

3. What products or services will the business provide?

   ____
   ____
   ____
   ____

4. Why are you starting the business?

   ____
   ____
   ____
   ____

5. What is your target market?

____
____
____
____

6. What is different about your business from the competitors?

____
____
____
____

7. How soon will the products or services be available?

____
____
____
____

8. How much startup money is needed for the business?

____
____
____
____

9. How long will it take to make a profit?

____
____
____
____

10. How will you market the business?

____
____
____
____

11. What promotions will you use for the business?

____
____
____

12. Where will your business be located?

13. What will be the legal structure of the business?

14. What vendors will you use?

15. How many employees will be needed?

16. What kind(s) of insurances will be needed?

17. How will your taxes get paid?

18. Do you like to make your own decisions?

____
____
____
____

19. Do you enjoy competition?

____
____
____
____

20. Do you have will power?

____
____
____
____

21. Are you, self-discipline? If yes, in what way?

____
____
____
____

22. Will you take advice from others?

____
____
____
____

23. Will you adapt to changes? Recently, what change did you have to adapt to?

____
____
____
____

24. Do you have the physical stamina to handle a business?

25. Do you have the emotional strength to handle a business?

26. Are you willing to work long hours?

27. Can you afford to lose your savings?

28. Do you have the skills, abilities, and expertise to be effective in business?

29. What are the two types of businesses?

30. Explain and differentiate the two types of businesses.

____

____

____

____

31. List 7 items that should be considered prior to opening a business from the above list.

____

____

____

____

____

____

____

Alright! You have made it through the questions. So, you see that there is a lot involved in being an entrepreneur or a small business owner. If you have not closed this book and decided to move forward, you can take one of the first steps and come up with a name for your business by contacting your local government. Then you need to find out if that name is available, and you must decide what products or services that you plan to sell, along with the prices. Your next step is to determine the mission and vision statements. A business for profit mission statement describes your purpose, along with what the company does for its customers, what the company does for its employees, and what the company does for its owners. A business for profit vision statement is a one-liner sentence statement describing the clear long term desired change resulting from the business influence. (See appendix for samples of both mission and vision statements.) After writing your mission and vision statements, then you will need to choose a business structure and you have several options, they are listed briefly below and you can research and obtain additional information and even consult an attorney to assist you in the correct business structure:

What is the difference between the mission & vision statements?
____
____
____
____

I. Business Structure

A. Sole Proprietor

A sole proprietor is a business which is owned and operated by an individual. The advantages of this form of organization include the ease in formation and freedom from government controls and restrictions. Disadvantages include less access to capital and financial resources. Also, this form of business structure provides less protection with regard to personal liability (if the owner's company should get into a position of owing more to others or company gets sued there is no protection against the owner's personal assets (*i.e.*, home, car etc.) may be required to be sold to pay the obligations of the business. Sole proprietor is usually registered with the county.

B. General Partnership

A general partnership is defined as two or more individuals carrying on an association as co-owners of a business for profit usually registered with the state in which the partnership will reside. Types of partnerships include general and limited. Before starting the company, the partners should agree on how much owner equity each will contribute, the extent to which each partner will work in the business, and which areas of operation will they be responsible for. In addition, you should never have a 50/50 partnership. Because once the honeymoon is over, it can get ugly, and you can wind up in court at the mercy of the judge. So, whoever idea it was to come up with the business should have the highest percentage so decide 50/48 and/or 60/40. Whatever the case, make sure that it is agreed upon and in writing. If the business is not successful and the partnership cannot pay all its debts, the general partnership may be required to do so using the owners' personal assets and resources.

C. Limited Liability Partnership

LLPs are organized to protect individual partners from personal liability for the negligent acts of other partners or employees not under their direct control. Partners report their share of profits and losses on their personal tax returns. This partnership consists of one or more general partners. The general partners manage the LLPs while typically the limited partners only have financial interest.

D. Limited Liability Company

A Limited Liability Company (LLC) is the non-corporate form of doing business that provides its owners with limited liability, flow-through tax treatment and operating flexibility through participation in management of the business. The LLC is well suited for every type of business venture except banking, insurance, which is prohibited by statute. Examples of acceptable businesses are: farming, agricultural, construction, manufacturing, transportation, retail, real estate and others. There are two types of LLCs. There is a general LLC that covers one business venture then you have the LLC that has multiple subdivisions under its umbrella. The LLC is usually registered with the state in which the company will reside.

E. Low-Profit Limited Liability Company

In the State of Illinois, you can investigate and see if the above holds true in the state in which your NFP resides. The above company was introduced January 2010 in which a company intends to qualify as a low-profit limited liability company pursuant to Section 1-26 of the Limited Liability Company Act and shall at all times, significantly further the accomplishment of one or more charitable or educational purposes as defined by the Internal Revenue Code (IRC).

F. C Corporations

A corporation is a distinct legal entity and is the most complex form of origination. A corporation may sell shares of stock, which are certificates indicating ownership, to as many people as is desirable. The shareholders then elect a board of directors, which elects a president and other officers who run the company on a day-to-day basis. Among the advantages of corporate formation are limited liability of the shareholders and the ease of transferring ownership. There are two types of corporations the C Corporation and the S corporation. Establishing either corporation in order to raise funds to start up the business the corporation can sell interest into the business in order to raise and have capital to operate. The corporations pay their shareholders what is known as dividends. Registration as a corporation will require Articles of Incorporation which must be filed with the Secretary of State indicating the purpose of the enterprise. And the corporation will be required to file annual reports with the Secretary of State. If the name of the business will include the word "Corporation", "INC.", "Incorporated" or "Corp." you must incorporate.

G. S Corporation

Electing S Corporation ("S Corp") status is an option that must be made through the Internal Revenue Service (IRS) when starting a business. In general, an S Corp passes through income and expenses to the shareholders, who then report them on their own income tax returns. To qualify for S Corp the corporation must meet several requirements one of which limits the number of shareholders to 75. All shareholders must consent to the corporation's choice of S Corp status. For, additional information you must contact the IRS department and the Secretary of State.

II. Other Business Options

A. Acquisitions

A common way to start a business is to acquire an existing business. Owners oftentimes are faced with retirement yet want the business to continue and family members do not want the responsibilities of continuing the business. Sometimes business owners die, and family members decide to sell the business, or the business could be up for sale for other reasons. Whatever the case proper registration, notice of sale/purchase of business assets, and obtaining a sales release of transferee liability must be completed. Contact your State Department of Revenue for additional information.

B. Franchise Disclosure

Buying into a franchise is usually a popular way of starting a business, and a Disclosure Act form need to be completed with both your State Attorney General and Secretary of State.

Once you have the business structures and licenses, you must make sure that if your industry requires professional licenses that they are registered with the Department of Financial and Professional Regulation ("DFPR") of your State. Acupuncturist, cosmetologist, massage therapist, and many others must register their professional licenses. Contact the DFPR of your state and see if your professional license must be registered as well. Now, if your industry is not regulated nor requires licensing you need to have certification or appropriate credentials to assure clients that you are well able to deliver the products and services that will be provided. In addition, many businesses are required to obtain permits and register with other state agencies.

1. What is the name of your business?

   ____

   ____

____
____

2. What are the several types of business structures?

____
____
____
____

3. Select a business structure that fits your goal.

____
____
____
____

4. Explain why you chose that particular business structure.

____
____
____
____

5. Do your business require professional licensing as well as a business operation license?

____
____
____
____

III.Business Plan

Once you have determined both a name and the business structure that you have opt for, then you need to develop a business plan. Usually, people that write these types of books have a business plan outlined tuck in an appendage. You will find a discussion of this topic right after the determination of the business structure above. Accomplishments should be in sequence, and it serves as a better guideline to help people from putting the cart before the horse. A business plan has several parts to it and each one is described below:

A. Business plan summary

Although this page is first, it is written once the business plan is completed. This section pretty much summarizes general information, target market, statistical data, promotion and marketing plans, etc.

B. Company & Industry

The purpose of this plan is to provide background information on your company, and to describe the condition and prospects of your industry. The following points should be covered:

The business you are operating or plan to operate, you should have the date or the projected startup date which includes a description of your products and/or services. Who are the current owners? What is the business structure selected? Who are the key principals and what are their roles within the business?

Give a brief explanation of your industry. In other words, what type of industry is your business (*e.g.*, restaurant, education, insurance, etc.). Then give a description of your major competitors and how are they performing in the industry in terms of growth, sales, and profits. You must also be able to give an analysis of the effect of major economic, social, technological, or regulatory trends.

C. Products and/or Services

Describe the products and/or services to be provided. Indicate the time and costs of the products and/or services. Describe any patent, copyrights, and/or other proprietary features. Discuss your advantages over your competitors and/or uniqueness that would make customers prefer you over others.

D. Market Analysis

You must determine if there is a need for your products and/or services in the market. You must identify your customers. Describe the target market customers are by age group, gender, and economic. If you developed a software, who would use it? House wives? Or millenniums?

In the business plan, describe the industry through statistical data with discussion reflecting the size of the market, development, and historical figures of the market. How has this industry performed? Also, in the business plan, you must give a projection of the market. What are the experts saying about the market within the industry? What will be the trend? Will there be market growth in five years, ten years, or twenty years?

Finally, under this section, you must describe your competitors and how they have performed in the market. What are your competitors' strengths and weaknesses? In this section, you must also describe your uniqueness and your marketing plans that make you stand head and shoulder above your competitors. The bottom line, the business plan must show that there is a need for your products and/or services. Make clear that you understand the needs of potential clients and will be able to meet those needs. Will you be able to sell products and/or services and make a profit?

E. Marketing Strategy

This section of the business plan requires you to provide the projections of sales, market share and target market, and to support your belief that your marketing plan will achieve projections. It should include the following:

- Estimated Sales and Market Share - Provide an estimate of sales and market shares (units and dollars) based on your assessment of customers or client acceptance of your products/services, potential market size and trends, and the competition. Also, identify any major customers who have made, or are willing to make purchase commitments.
- Market Strategy – Identify your target market(s). It is important to target and/or segment your market carefully concentrating

your resources on the needs of a specific segment and carving out a market niche may mean the difference between success and failure. Also, outline your method of identifying and contacting potential customers or clients as well as the product or service features that will be emphasized.

- Pricing – Discuss the prices to be charged for your products and/or services and determine how the company's pricing compares to major competitors. Your pricing does not have to be the same as your competitors. However, you must be capable of explaining why your business is different. Remember consumers will comparatively shop. You should also note that most consumers equate high pricing with higher quality product and service. Explain how your pricing or fee structure will enable you to gain acceptance of your products and/or services, maintain and increase market share, and provide for a profit.
- Sales and Distribution – Discuss your plans for selling and distribution. If a direct salesforce will be used, describe how it will be organized and controlled. This should include the number and location of sales personnel and the salary or commission each will receive. If distributors or sales representatives will be used, describe how they will be recruited and paid and what geographic territories will be covered. Also, you could discuss sales efficiency issues such as how many sales calls it will take to get an order and how large an average order will be.
- Service and Warranty Issues – Discuss your service and warranty policies and your methods for handling service and warranty problems.
- Promotion – Discuss how you will generate awareness of your products and/or services, including the use of such tactics as trade show participation, trade periodical ads, promotional literature, public rationalism, social media, web logging (blogging) application software (apps), etc. Estimate the percentage of total expenses that will be allocated to promotion and when such expenses are likely to be included.

F. Operations

In this section, you should describe how you plan to produce or perform your services, including how and where it will be carried out, your physical space and equipment needs, and your labor requirements. Include the following information:

- Location – Describe the location of the business and the advantages and disadvantages of the site with respect to labor and material costs and availability, proximity to customers, access to transportation, state and local laws (including zoning) and utility costs.
- Physical Space and Equipment – Describe the physical facilities in use or to be acquired (leased, purchased, or built) and the costs and timing of such acquisitions. Estimate future facilities and equipment needs based on sales projections, including the cost of additional capacity and its timing.
- Production Processes – Describe the production processes necessary to develop your products or provide your services, including method of production, procedures for quality, production, inventory control, raw materials required (including sources, costs, etc.), organization and control of purchases, breakdown of fixed production costs, and breakdown of variable unit costs by products and/or services.
- Labor – Other than management, describe to what extent the local labor force is adequate in terms of quality and quantity. If applicable, discuss the type of training needed and the cost to your company.

G. Management and Organization

The experience training and talent of your management team is very important, particularly if you are seeking equity financing. Generally, venture capital firms will conduct a complete reference check of each member of your management team. Therefore, this section of your business plan should describe the following:

- Organization – Explain how your company's management team is organized and describe the primary role of each team member. If appropriate, include an organizational chart. Demonstrate how team members' skills complement each other. Investors are looking for a team with a balance of management, financial production and marketing skills as well as experience with the products and/or services you intend to provide.

- Key Management – Prepare a brief summary of each key member of the management team to include duties and responsibilities, career highlights, and significant accomplishments (include resumes in the appendix). The discussion of the management team should also outline any weaknesses and how they will be overcome (*e.g.*, training, recruiting outside advisors, etc.).
- Compensation of Ownership – Indicate how each member of the management team will be compensated (*e.g.*, salary, profit sharing, incentive bonus, stock options, etc.) and what investment each has in the company including a list of key stockholders with the number of shares each owns.
- Board of Directors – Identify your board members, briefly discuss how they are expected to benefit your company and list their investment in the company if any.
- Professional Services – List the legal, accounting, banking and any other service organization that will advise your company or help fill gaps in the organization.

H. Schedule of activities

A realistic schedule that shows the timing of activities for the major events of your business plan is critical to your company's success. It also indicates the ability of management to plan the company's development. A schedule should be prepared outlining steps to be taken in your company's development and the completion date of each step for a period of three to five years. Entrepreneurs tend to underestimate the amount of time needed to complete various tasks. Be realistic.

I. Critical Risks and Problems

The development and operation of any business involves risks and problems, and it is best to identify these potentially negative factors and explore their implications. To determine the risks and problems that require discussion, you should identify the plan assumptions or potential problems that are most critical in terms of the success of your venture. Then discuss them and outline possible ways for dealing with them or minimizing their impact.

J. Financial information

The amount of financial information needed in your business plan will depend on the stage of financing, the amount of money needed, and the nature of financing being sought. Generally, the amount of information required will increase as the amount of financing requested increases, as it will when equity (versus fully collateralized) lending is requested.

Your business plan should describe, in general terms, the type and amount of funding you are seeking. Also, information on your company's present financial status (include current financial statements if you are already in operation) and financial projections must be included. This part of the financial information section should cover the following:

- Desired Financing – State how much money is needed and how it will be used.
- Capitalization – Explain the capital structure of your company and what effect funding will have.
- Use of Funds – Explain how you plan to use the funds. The use should be consistent with your financial projections for example. If you need seed capital, you might indicate that the money will be used to further develop your product and set up a marketing organization. In subsequent rounds of financing you can refer the reader to your financial projections for details, but briefly explain how much of the money will be used for research, development, production, equipment, etc.
- Future Financing – Clearly outline your company's future funding needs. Discuss when you will require future funding and what the milestones are for reaching that point.

- Current Financial Statements – If your company has a track record, provide financial statements for the last three years or from inception.
- Financial Projections – You should provide a three-year cash flow, projected income (profits and losses) statements and balance sheet projections. If your company has been in business for a while, the cash flow projections should be on a quarterly basis for the first year and annually thereafter. Otherwise, cash flow projections should be on a month-to-month basis for the first year, a quarterly basis for the second year and annually thereafter. When making financial projections, it is mandatory that you explain all key assumptions. They can get involved, so make use of your accountant and/or other professional advisors. There are also several good computer software packages available to help you accomplish these tasks.

Your financial projections and funding request must be keyed to your market expectations. You should begin your financial projections with a sales forecast. Often, entrepreneurs make the mistake of starting at the production cost level with the assumption that everything produced can be marketed for a profit. Starting with a sales forecast will also help you define how much cash you will have coming from operations and when it will be coming in. This is essential to forecasting cash flow and determining how much equity and debt capital you will require until the company generates a positive cash flow.

You may want to seek assistance from an accountant, Score, Small Business Administration, or Small Business Development Centers.

In summary, your plan should describe:

- Your company and industry,
- The product and/or service,
- The market and marketing approach,
- How the product or service will be produced,
- Management of the company, and

- How much money the company needs and what it will do with it.

By following these guidelines, you should be able to describe your company and its market niche, your operations strategy, and future goals and objectives. Your business plan will also be able to provide a prospective investor or lender with information about your company that is well prepared and persuasive in showing the potential of your business.

1. What is a business plan?

____

____

____

____

2. What industry is your business in?

____

____

____

____

3. What are the various parts of the business plan?

____

____

____

____

4. What products and/or services you intent to offer?

____

____

____

____

5. Describe your target population.

____

____

____

____

6. How did you identify the target population?

____

____

____

____

7. Describe your target population demographics.

____

____

____

____

8. How will you market your business?

____

____

____

____

9. How will the products and/or services be produced?

____

____

____

____

10. List the management team.

____

____

____

____

11. How much money will be required for business startup?

____

____

____

____

12. How do you intend to raise the capital for business startup?

____

____

____

____

IV. Registration

After developing and submitting your business plan and obtaining financing, then you need to acquire your business license and make sure this is included in the business plan. If you have a brick and mortar establishment whatever licenses, registrations, and permits need to be acquired then you must obtain those items as well (day care centers, restaurants, hair salons, etc.). You can contact your municipal offices for additional information as well as the Secretary of State in which the business will reside. You must have your licenses listed with the DFPR. There is a listing of those professions which must have licenses and be registered with their offices that you can obtain. (*e.g.*, pharmacist, cosmetologist, embalmer, etc.). If your business does not require a license, perhaps an accreditation or certification is sufficient. It is realistic that you should have some type of credential in opening your business that will reflect your experience and education in the industry, which will assure the clients/customers that they will receive the services desired. However, many have gone into business and didn't have the education or experience, but they hired people with the licenses and /or credentials and they just deemed themselves as the CEO.

1. What is the next step after developing your business plan?

   ____

   ____

   ____

   ____

2. Do your business require registrations? If so, list the office to contact for registration procedure.

   ____

   ____

   ____

   ____

3. Do your business require permits? If so, list the office to contact to request permit(s).

____
____
____
____

4. Do your business require you to have a professional license and registration? If so, where do you go to obtain the information needed?

____
____
____
____

A. Environmental Standards

Every business needs to contact the small business environmental assistance program to determine if any requirements are expected of the business. The contact is kept confidential and its purpose is to help businesses to understand their environmental obligations.

Why does every business need to contact the small business environment assistance program?

____
____
____

B. Taxes

Taxation for small businesses can be quite simple or very complex, depending on the size, business structure, and type of operation. Check with your state on the taxes that are required. You can also contact an attorney and tax professional as well. In the State of Illinois, you are required to pay an income tax. Every individual, partnership, corporation, trust, and estate residing in Illinois earning or receiving income in Illinois must pay an income tax based on net income. A replacement tax is also applied to the next income of partnerships, corporations, and trusts. S corporation are subject only to replacement tax. You must also pay federal taxes. Below is additional information for each business structures but once again consult an Attorney and/or tax professional.

- Sole Proprietorship – A sole proprietor must pay individual income taxes on earnings from the business.
- Partnerships and Limited Liability Companies – Each partner/owner must pay taxes on the distribute share of partnership/owner's income. In addition, Illinois has a replacement tax that applies to partnership. You have to find out your state requirement.
- Corporation – The corporation entity must pay a corporate income tax and replacement tax, which is administered and collected by the Department of Revenue of your state. In addition, corporations are assessed a franchise tax each year based on their paid-in capital and a corporate personal property tax replacement income tax. Corporate and franchise taxes are administered and collected by the Secretary of State's Office.

1. What is the tax requirement for your business?

____

____

____

____

2. Where can you go to seek help in determining your tax status?

____

____

____

____

C. Sales Tax (Check with your State)

The use tax is imposed directly on the purchaser for the privilege of using and consuming tangible personal property that has been purchased anywhere.

Retailers are required to pay the Retailer Occupation Tax and, by law reimburse themselves for the tax collecting Use Tax from customers based on the selling price of the tangible personal property. The business can keep 1.75 per cent of the taxes collected for acting as an agent.

The service occupation tax is imposed directly on the receipts from the selling price of any tangible personal property transferred as part of a sale of service if the cost to the service person is 35% or more of the total charged.

Now, there are some instances where there are sales tax exemptions for businesses. You may contact your State Department of Revenue to inquire information regarding the subject matter.

1. What are sale taxes?

    ____
    ____
    ____
    ____

2. Which businesses are required to pay sale taxes?

    ____
    ____
    ____
    ____

3. Where would you go to find out about sale taxes for your business?

    ____
    ____
    ____
    ____

D. <u>Property Taxes</u>

If you have a brick and mortar business location, then you will have the option of leasing or owning a physical location. If you own a building, then you are required to pay property taxes. The property tax rate is determined by local taxing district and is paid to the township or county tax collector in the year of the following assessment. There are some businesses that are online in the form of websites, Facebook, and ecommerce in which customers can download or order desired products at one point no taxes were required, but recently business owners had to include taxes along with the shipping and handling process.

1. What options do you have in term of physical location for your business?

 ____

 ____

2. Who determines the property taxes?

 ____

 ____

3. Are online businesses required to pay taxes? If so, which?

 ____

 ____

E. Withholding Taxes

Certain taxes must be withheld from employee wages and remitted to the government (IRS and others). These include state and federal income taxes and FICA (Social Security and Medicaid). You may be required to register with both the federal government and the State in which your business resides for tax withholding purposes. You may want to contact a bank or tax professional for assistance.

1. What taxes should be withheld from an employee?

 ____

 ____

2. Who should you contact to discuss the withholding of employee taxes?

 ____

____
____
____

F. Employer Identification Number

Every business entity except a sole proprietorship must have an EIN (also known as a Federal Tax Identification Number) to use as its tax payer identification number. A sole proprietorship must also have an EIN if it:

- Pays wages to one or more employees, or
- Files any excise tax returns, including those for alcohol, tobacco, or firearms.

Otherwise, sole proprietors can use their Social Security Number as their business Tax Payer Identification Number. To apply for an EIN, use form SS-4 application for Employer Identification Number from the Internal Revenue Service.

1. What is an Employer Identification Number?

____
____
____
____

2. How do you obtain an Employer Identification Number (EIN)?

____
____
____
____

G. Immigration Reform and Control Act

Federal law requires that every employer and agricultural recruiter/referrer-for-a-fee hiring or recruiting/referring-for-a-fee an individual for employment in the United States to complete a Form I-9. Employment eligibility verification form will help you verify your employee's identity and employment authorization.

Employers must keep each I-9 on file for at least three years or one year after the employment ends, whichever is longer. As of April 2005, employers may sign and store I-9 Forms electronically.

Employment related immigration regulations and procedures are based on legislation passed by Congress and can be complex. To assist employers, United States Citizenship and Immigration Services have structured a wide range of information to inform employers on employment statutes and regulations, employees' rights, preventing discrimination, training, and related immigration subjects.

What form is required to prove your United States citizenship?

____

H. Employee Leasing Company/Professional Employer Organization

An employee leasing company or professional employer organization provides human resources solution incorporating employee benefits, payroll, worker's compensation, recruiting, risk/safety management, training and development. They also provide state and federal regulatory compliance assistance for small business owners, as well as healthcare, and are required to register with the department of insurance within your designated state.

Hiring, managing, and paying employees can be time-consuming distraction from major business concerns. Business owners contract with Professional Employer Organization ("PEO") to assume these duties and responsibilities. PEOs have experienced staff in these areas which take away the burden of these concerns and allow the small business to grow by improving their productivity and profitability as they focus on their mission. These are full service PEOs and payroll service only PEOs. Employers can choose which service best suits their business needs.

What is the importance of a leasing/professional employer organization and what is the benefit of using their services?

____

____

____

____

I. Child Support

Federal and state laws require judges in domestic relations cases to order employers to withhold a portion of an employee's income for payment of child support. The order is mandatory in cases involving people who receive assistance from the Department of Human Services. When an income withholding notice is served on the employer, the employer withholds the amount stated and sends the amount withheld to the state disbursement unit. If employers fail to do so as required, then the employer will be liable for the amount due and cited to pay a fine.

An employer may not discharge, discipline, deny employment or otherwise penalize an employee because he/she is subject to an income withholding notice. An employer who does so will be required to reinstate the employee and will be fined.

J. Workers' Compensation

By law an employer is required to provide insurance for employees' accidental deaths, injuries and occupational diseases arising out of and in the course of employment. The insurance requirement is applicable to almost all businesses and must include provisions for all medical expenses, rehabilitation and retraining, temporary and total disability, permanent disability, and death benefits. Insurances generally is purchased through private firms or agents, although businesses can apply to the commission for permission to self-insure. Annual premiums are based on total company payroll, loss experience and type of business. Employers must post a notice in the workplace listing the insurance carrier and explaining workers' rights under the law. Temporary workers who otherwise do not receive any company benefits are still provided workers' compensation.

If you are refused coverage by two or more companies, you can obtain insurance from the assigned risk pool. Rates will be approximately 20% higher than the open market.

K. Department of Employment Security

Employers may also register a newly created business with the Department of Employment Security. You may also be required to make unemployment insurance contributions to the department. Generally, you are liable for such contributions if you have:

- Paid at least $1500 in wages in a single calendar quarter or employed one or more persons for 20 weeks in a given calendar year,
- Paid at least $1,000 in cash wages in one calendar quarter for domestic work, or
- Paid at least $20,000 in cash wages in one calendar quarter or employed 10 or more workers for 20 weeks in a given calendar year for farm work.

When are you required to register your business with the department of employment security?

____

____

____

____

L. Occupational Safety and Health Administration

Employers are responsible for providing a safe and healthful workplace for their employees. The OSHA role is to assure the safety and health of American workers by setting and enforcing standards, providing training, outreach, and education; establishing partnerships and encouraging continual improvement in workplace safety and health OSHA rules for recording and reporting occupational injuries and illnesses affect 1.4 million establishments. Small businesses with ten or fewer employees throughout the year are exempt from most of the requirements of the OSHA recordkeeping rules, as are a number of specific industries in the retail, service, finance, insurance, and real estate sectors that are classified as low-hazard. The OSHA recordkeeping system has five steps that are outlined in their Small Business Handbook. An employer is required to report to OSHA within eight hours of the accident all work-related fatalities or multiple hospitalizations that involve three or more employees.

Employers are required to continually display a poster prepared by the U.S. Department of Labor that informs employees of their rights under OSHA. The poster, which is available in different languages, must be displayed in a conspicuous place where employees can see it. Private employers may use the poster available from OSHA's website or a suitable reproduction or facsimile. OSHA's posters are free of charge. The Industrial Services Office of the Department of Labor offers free, confidential pre-inspection consultation services, which are designed to prevent citations and penalties resulting from the actual federal OSHA inspection. Consultants assist employers in complying with OSHA workplace safety and health standards in developing a complete safety and health program to eliminate employee lost time, production downtime, and material damage in their operation.

The federal and state laws also require that other posters be displayed on business premises to inform employees of their rights and benefits. These posters may be obtained at no cost from the Department of Labor.

M. Equal Employment Opportunity Commission (EEOC)

The law requires an employer to post notices describing the Federal law prohibiting job discrimination based on race, color, sex, national origin, religion, age equal pay, disability, and genetic information, EEOC's poster entitle "Equal Employment Opportunity is the Law" is available in English, Arabic, Chinese, and Spanish. You may order up to five copies from their website. Businesses with 15 or more employees must display this poster.

N. U.S. Department of Labor (USDOL)

Businesses with one or more employees must display certain posters to inform employees of their rights. Some of the statutes and regulations enforced by agencies within the U.S. Department of Labor require that posters or notices be posted in the workplace. USDOL provides electronic copies of the required posters and some of the posters are available in languages other than English.

1. What is OSHA?

   ____
   ____
   ____
   ____

2. What is OSHA's goal for the work place?

   ____
   ____
   ____
   ____

3. When is a business exempt from OSHA requirements?

   ____
   ____
   ____
   ____

O. Workers' Compensation Commission

Employers must display a workplace notice listing the insurance carrier and explaining workers' rights under the Workers' Compensation Act.

What is the workers' compensation commission?

____
____
____
____

P. Department of Labor (DOL)

Workplace Notice requires employers to display the poster entitled "Notice to Employers and Employees" DOL is responsible for enforcement of laws which protect workers. These laws provide a workplace in which employer and employee are each bound by the same impartial laws and standards.

What notices do the Department of Labor require employers to post?

____
____
____
____

V. Business Services

A. Obtaining Legal Counsel

Many business owners consider legal services only when their firms are in trouble. However, costly and time-consuming legal problems can be averted by retaining a competent attorney who can advise on such business areas as choosing the type of business organization that best suits your needs and objectives, protecting your family's financial security from the business risks advising you as to local, state, and federal regulations which affect your business, obtaining financing, and giving practical advice on many business problems. Attorneys also can provide professional help when dealing with other parties such as financial institutions, owners of possible store or plant locations, union officials, governmental bodies, franchising companies, contracts with suppliers, and customers and insurance coverage negotiation with employees.

In addition, other problems may arise requiring the services of an attorney. For instance, the employer may be served with wage deduction orders against employees, which-if not handled properly-can result in personal liability on the part of the employer. Other examples:

- The business may face collection problems with its customers,
- The business may become involved in disputes with its trade creditors,
- The business may dispute with both present and former employers, and
- The business may have expansion opportunities or restructuring may need to be reconsidered.

When seeking an attorney's counsel or assistance, be as prepared as possible. Collect pertinent data, do necessary research, and have as much information as possible about your business. This will save your attorney time and save you money. When considering an attorney, use discretion. Remember an attorney will provide services fundamental to the success of your business.

For help with legal issues, you may contact Legal Aid. Legal Aid's mission is to increase access to justice for lower-income, vulnerable residents, and businesses through innovative use of technology to assist and educate the public.

One of Legal Aid's goals is to serve as the central depository of legal services. They reduce the time it takes applicants to secure services and direct them to the best provider to meet their legal needs. They also offer live online legal assistance and searching capabilities.

1. Should a business seek legal counsel?
   Yes ________ No ________

2. If so, how can a business owner obtain counsel?

____
____
____
____

B. Insurance Coverage

Many people starting a small business fail to consider their insurance needs. A well-planned insurance program is essential for protecting a business from unforeseen losses and significant financial burdens. Four types of insurance coverages are essential: fire, liability, vehicle, and workers' compensation. In addition, there are several desirable types of insurance coverage: business interruption, crime, key employee, Officer and Director, and home office. In organizing an insurance program, there are four basic considerations:

- Recognize Your Risks - Recognize the perils facing the business and the potential loss from each.
- Study Insurance Costs - Before purchasing insurance, investigate the methods by which you can reduce the cost of coverage. This includes shopping for the appropriate insurance plans.
- Have a Plan - Prepare an insurance plan that is compatible with the operation and goals of the business.
- Get Professional Advice - A qualified insurance agency, producer, broker, or consultant can explain options, recommend the best coverage, and help save money.

1. What are several types of insurance?

____
____
____
____

2. Why should a business be insured?

____

____

____

____

C. Bookkeeping

You must keep sound financial records. Below are somethings to consider while in the process of developing your system:

- Starting and keeping an accounting system for the accurate and timely recording of the company's cash receipts, disbursements, sales, and operating expenses.
- Preparing periodic statements, which includes statement of assets and liabilities as of a given date (balance sheet), statement of results or operations for a given period of time (income statement), statement of changes in financial positions, and establishment of systems that track accounts receivable and payments due.
- Preparing state and federal income tax returns, and
- Preparing social security, withholding, property, and other tax returns.

These responsibilities may be undertaken from within or outside of the business. This will depend on the size and nature of the business and your own experience and available time. Your accountant, attorney, or banker can help decide your needs for a bookkeeper or bookkeeping service.

D. Accounting

In addition to bookkeeping requirements, you may need the services of a certified public accountant (CPA), an accountant who has passed a written examination prepared by the American Institute of Certified Public Accountants and who has received a state license for their public practice of accounting. CPAs provide the following services:

- Auditing- Although you may have hired a bookkeeper to maintain accounting records and prepare financial statements, there are many reasons why you may need financial statements certified by a CPA. For example, banks and other lenders frequently require an audit before a loan is granted and during the period that the loan is outstanding.
- Taxes- Most businesses do not have employees who are experts in tax matters and, therefore, must rely on professional assistance. This is particularly true today when the tax laws are complex and continually changing. The tax service provided by CPAs include planning transactions for the lowest present and future tax liabilities, preparation of tax returns, and estate planning.
- Consulting- Because of their experience with many companies in many industries. CPAs may be able to assist you in cost reduction, improvement of reports, installing or upgrading accounting systems, budgeting and forecasts, financial analyses, production control, quality control, compensation or personnel, and records management.

The independent Accountants Association established in 1949 also can refer a competent accountant to the small business person. The membership is derived of both CPA and non-CPA accountants. Many accountants are licensed to represent a client before the IRS. However, non-CPA accountants can assist with accounting, sales, payroll tax preparation, and other business consulting needs.

1. Why should a business owner seek an Accountant?

   ____

   ____

   ____

   ____

2. How can hiring an Accountant help a business?

   ____

   ____

____
____

3. What type of services do an Accountant offers?
____
____
____
____

4. Can a business person rely upon a Bookkeeper?
____
____
____
____

5. What is a Bookkeeper?
____
____
____
____

E. Online Small Business Training

You can enhance your knowledge and boost your business skills easily with online E-Training that is both cost-effective and convenient. Instead of rearranging your busy schedule or missing out on work or family time for a traditional classroom course, you can learn whenever and wherever you want. Courses cover a wider range of business topics including business planning, marketing/sales, legal fundamentals and technology. Our entraining courses are the same as regular instructor-led courses because they are taught by certified instructors with a small business background. These experts have created a dynamic curriculum for each of the courses, so you receive a high quality educational experience when you want it.

If you do not understand a topic or need additional information you can schedule a counseling session free of charge at a Small

Business Development Center. The convenience of attending an online training session cannot be overstated.

Another online Small Business Resource is Business USA.gov which is a federal website which offers entrepreneurs and small businesses a direct path to information on financing, exporting, starting and growing a business, veteran's programs, and disaster assistance. They also offer step-by-step guides to help identify business opportunities, access financing, learn about taxes, and understand the new healthcare changes and laws.

You can check if your State has a joblink.com which is an internet-based job board, which allows businesses to post help-wanted ads for free. It is quickly becoming the state's go-to resource for employers to find that next employee. It provides the ability to search for specific skills. The no-cost, HR-recruitment effort will even help businesses identify potential tax breaks associated with certain hires, such as veterans.

F. Business/Trade/Professional Associations

There are associations to represent every business/trade/and professional Associations which is engaged in the promoting of business interests of their members and often conduct research, provide educational services, develops statistics, sponsor quality education and certification standards, lobby public officials, and publish newsletters, books, and periodicals. Benefits may include certification, free attendance at trade shows and conventions, workshops and seminars, dollar-saving bankcards, promote public awareness of the value and diversity; and, in some instances, insurances. The smaller business owner has little time to lobby government officials on issues of interest (or perhaps how to even go about it), which makes a membership in an association a valuable aspect of operating a business, especially if your profession/trade is heavily regulated. Additional benefits include the networking with people in your field of interest and keeping up with industry trends and developments.

How can small business training benefit a business owner?

____
____
____
____

G. Chambers of Commerce

Chambers of Commerce Acts in much the same way as associations and offer many of the same programs. Chambers, however, support the entire concept of a community and market the area as a whole, which includes its businesses, churches, schools, parks and recreation, special events, historical significance, natural environment, and other civic amenities. Benefits of membership in a chamber include opportunities to network and create an awareness of business name, product or service. By getting involved in chamber activities, members have the opportunity to meet and work with area business leaders on issues impacting not only businesses, but also the area. Chambers work to improve the economy, community, and businesses.

How can a business owner benefit from being associated with a chamber of commerce?

____
____
____
____

VI. Resources

A. Governmental Grants

There is greatly exaggerated publicity, as well as many dishonest schemes, surrounding the topic of government grants for small businesses. First and foremost, information regarding grants can be obtained free of charge. If you are being charged a fee to receive information, then you should disregard the source. Grant information is free. And if you apply for grants and obtain one it is also free. You do not pay back a grant. However, there are limited amount of governmental grants. The grants are most commonly available for non-profit and educational organizations or for very specific purposes (*i.e.*, clean energy development and small business innovation research).

Most states do not provide grants for starting or expanding a business, paying off debt, or covering operational expenses nor does the US Small Business Administration (SBA). Grants from the federal government are authorized and appropriated through bills passed by Congress and signed by the president. The grant authority varies widely among agencies.

The fastest, easiest, and most comprehensive method of finding small business grants, loans and other financing options offered by federal and state government is to use the SBA Loans and Grants Search Tool. When you use this tool, it is not necessary to select a specific industry from the search criteria list. Also, if you have all of the selection criteria blank and simply select a state, the tool will show you all grants, loans, and other financing opportunities available to all types of businesses in that state.

Another option to search for grants is via Grants.gov. This website houses the federal government's searchable public database of information for over 1,000 grant programs which provide access to annual awards approximately at $500 Billion.

Most people start businesses from monies saved for it in their accounts. Then there been those that received support through family members and friends. Then people have been known to use their credit cards to finance the startup of their business(es). There are very few grants that can be used for startup purposes it like looking for a needle in a hay stack. If you are seeking "free money" to launch or expand your business, you would be better off focusing your efforts on developing a sound business plan that capitalizes on a viable market, a compelling product or service, and a passion for business. You can also seek to sell shares of your business to raise capital, and even seek angel investors.

If you find a grant for your business and is eligible for a governmental grant, it is important for you to know that the government will often expect a return on the grant, either indirectly through improvement in regional economies or directly through the development of technology which the government can use in its programs and services.

List ways that business owners can generate funding for business ventures:

1. ____
2. ____
3. ____
4. ____
5. ____
6. ____
7. ____

B. Obtaining Financing

Financial resources available to small businesses can vary, depending on whether you are starting a new business or purchasing an existing business. The most common source of financing for a small business is personal resources. Many businesses begin on a 'shoestring" or household budget until their financial situation and cash flow are stable. Once again friends, relatives and financial institutions also are potential sources of financing. Business loans for startup enterprises are not easily obtained, but fortunately there are various alternatives to consider.

C. <u>How to Apply For a Loan:</u>

The following guidelines should be used for the current or prospective business owner when preparing to request financial assistance.

Those who seek to start a business should consider the following:

- Describe the type of business you plan to establish,
- Submit information on the products or services the business plans to offer and identify existing and potential customers and competitors,
- Describe your experience and management capabilities,
- Prepare an estimate of how much you or others have to invest in the business and how much will you need to borrow,
- Prepare a current financial statement (balance sheet) listing all personal assets and all liabilities,
- Prepare a detailed projection of earnings for the first three years the business will operate,
- List collateral to be offered as security for the loan, indicating your estimate of the present market value of each item, and
- State the amount of the loan and exact purpose(s) for which it can be used.

Those who are currently operating a business(es) should:

- Submit a brief history of the business and its employment growth.
- Submit information on your company's products and/or services and identify existing and potential major customers and competitors.
- Prepare a current financial statement (balance sheet) listing all assets and liabilities of the business.
- Have a earnings (profit and loss) statement for the last two years and for the current period to the date of the balance sheet.

- Prepare a current personal financial statement of the owner, each partner, or each stockholder owing 20% or more of the corporate stock in the business.
- List collateral to be offered as security for the loan, with an estimate of the present market value of each item, and
- State the amount of the loan requested and exact purposes for which it can be used.

Along with the proceeding information, a business plan should be submitted to the lender, outlining the basic structure and direction of the business.

What are the requirements to receive financing from a financial institution?

____
____
____
____
____
____
____
____
____
____

D. Banking Services

Businesses have special needs and the types of commercial accounts available vary differently as those for individuals. Work with your local banker to discuss the following banking services.

E. Commercial Checking Accounts

Checking account services are available for every size of business, with custom check designs and a variety of check formats that provide audit controls for the account. Service charges may be calculated on the number of checks written and the number of checks deposited plus a monthly maintenance fee. In most cases, an account receives a monthly earnings credit based on an average of previous weeks. Treasury bill rates which is applied against the service charges calculated for the account. Also, you must have an Employer Identification Number to operate a commercial checking account. There may be other requirements as well.

F. Commercial Deposit Services

Commercial bulk deposits allow the business to process bulk change, pick up currency, or drop off large deposits. Also, with the 24-hour automatic teller facilities, businesses and individuals have greater access to certain banking services. Federal tax depository services also are available to help prevent a penalty for late payment of taxes. The date the bank accepts the deposit establishes the date of payment.

G. Commercial Savings/Investment Services

Business saving programs allows a business to deposit up to a certain amount in a saving account that earns interest on a percentage per year, compound continuously for an effective yield. Short-term investments also are available using Certificates of Deposit and Repurchase Agreement. Online banking is available, as well.

H. Online Banking

Online banking also known as E-banking or internet banking allows customers of a financial institution (bank credit union, etc.) the ability to conduct financial transactions on a secure website, which is operated by the financial institution. Registration for the service is required with the financial institution. Upon registration, access is given to online banking through the financial institution's website.

I. Loan Services

In some instances, the bank can provide assistance in obtaining and financing loans. The following are some possible areas of assistance:

- Working capital loans provide short-term access to interim operating funds.
- A revolving line of credit is a pre-established borrowing limit that can help meet monthly expenses.
- Inventory financing or a seasonal line of credit can help see the business through crucial, capital-intensive periods, which are common to agriculture and certain types of wholesale and retail operations.
- A letter of credit from a bank can improve purchasing power in business transactions outside the local area.
- Account receivable financing allows borrowing against business already on the books.
- Equipment financing and leasing arrangements can help to properly equip the business or expand it when it is ready to grow.
- Capital loans provide funds to help start or invest in a commercial enterprise.
- Real estate mortgages are available to help acquire property and real estate management services can help manage the property.
- Credit investigations can help protect the business owner when dealing with unfamiliar sources.

Briefly, in an overview, describe the various banking services and list below those services that are applicable for your type of business:

____

____

____

____
____
____
____
____
____
____
____
____

Why were those services chosen?

____
____
____
____

J. Credit Card Service

In this age of plastic, most businesses accept major credit cards as payment for services or products. A local bank can make your business accessible to the Visa, MasterCard, American Express, and other credit systems. When contacting a bank which handles those accounts, you will be asked to provide commercial and financial statements, and the bank will do an analysis of the business solvency. If unable to estimate the business income, a personal credit check will be conducted to ascertain dependability. Upon approval, the bank will establish a commercial account for the business into which you deposit the credit card "bank" copies. The bank receives statements from the credit card company and remits payment from your account. Each bank imposes a processing cost on the business account depending upon average sales and volume. This can be anywhere from two to three percent-usually the former. The bank and the credit card company can either rent or sell one or more credit card machines. At some point the business may want to consider more sophisticated equipment which automatically determines the validity of a credit card. After signing an agreement with the bank, the business will receive monthly statements of account balance.

K. Debit Card Service

A debit card (also known as bank card or check card) is also a method for payment of services and products. Debit cards provide the cardholder electronic access to his or her bank account at a financial institution. Unlike credit cards, payments using a debit card are immediately transferred from the cardholder's designated bank account, instead of them paying for the product or service at a later date.

What are the similarities and differences between a business credit card service and a business debit card service?

BUSINESS CREDIT CARD SERVICES	BUSINESS DEBIT CARD SERVICES

List the one(s) you chose to use for banking purposes below:

____

____

____

____

____

____

____

L. Check Cashing Protection

A business can enhance its profits by welcoming a potential customer's check, but along with a check cashing policy comes the built-in risk of receiving a bad check. No business is immune. There are several ways; however, to be protected as possible when providing this service.

It is sound policy to have the check writer include their phone, driver's license, and social security numbers on the check. The check should have the person's name and address pre-printed. In case of problems, the writer can be reached.

In order to verify if a check is good at point of purchases, several companies provide a tracking system and can tell a subscribing member (generally via an 800 number) whether or not to accept a check. For a one-time enrollment fee, a sales representative will explain the service and provide training for employees on how to use the system. Thereafter, a monthly fee entitles you to check verification and guaranteed payment if the service indicates a check is good that subsequently is not.

There also are check-cashing protection systems that will guarantee, up to a certain limit all bad checks you receive. Acting as a type of insurance agency, the systems charge a monthly rate based on the average volume of checks you receive and provide personalized service.

When you receive an "insufficient" or non-sufficient funds" (ISF/NSF) check returned by a bank, you have several recourses:

- Wait a reasonable amount of time and redeposit the check,
- Contact the individual who wrote the check requesting that they make the check good, and
- Post a notice alerting employees not to accept checks from the individual until the outstanding check is made good.

If satisfaction has not been received within a reasonable amount of time, send a written demand to the person's last known address by certified letter, return receipt requested. By law, the individual who fails to pay the amount of the written check within 30 days is liable for triple the amount owed but not less than $100 or more than $500, plus attorney's fees and court costs for recovery. Every state has its own law for court costs for recovery.

In order to bring a civil suit in small claims or other appropriate court, you will need a copy of the letter, certified mail receipt, a copy of the check (front and back), and a letter from the bank indicating that the check is no good. Another course of action would be to contact the local State's Attorney's Office. The State's Attorney's office may contact the maker of the check by letter to finally resolve any questions of inadvertence or may initiate prosecution immediately. Upon initial contact with the State's Attorney's Office, you will be asked to complete an incident report to aid in prosecution of the case. Remember that most people do not set out to defraud or pass bogus checks, but there are enough who do, so remain alert. The local police department may be a source of assistance if forgery is suspected.

How can a business owner protect the business from fraudulent checks?

____

____

____

____

M. <u>Other Services</u>

The nature of banking is such that it lends itself readily to other services. Following are some of the other services offered by banks:

- Business advice – It frequently is said that the banker should be a business guide and friend to his clients. Bank officers develop a broad understanding of the operations of their clients' businesses. Some banks employ engineering and management experts, who are made available to their clients for suggestions and guidance. It is very important to find a banker who is interested in you and your company.

- Credit advice – Every sizable bank has a credit department that handles problems that arise daily. A bank with a good credit department frequently can be helpful to the business owner.
- Agent services – Although it may act as an agent in many important and complex ways, the use of a bank as an agent for collection and disbursement services of various kinds can be of invaluable assistance to smaller businesses.
- Trust Services – Most banks have trust departments that, among other things, handle financial affairs for people who want them to manage or hold investments and to collect income and pay it out as agreed. Also, many times a bank is named as executor in a will to take charge when an individual dies.
- Safe deposit boxes – Many banks provide safe deposit box services. The service is a simple one and is frequently used for safekeeping of various business records.

Identify and list other business services that are offered by a bank that you may take advantage of to grow your business below:

____

____

____

____

____

____

____

____

N. Investing Profits

Because it can be difficult to anticipate volume and a general unwillingness exists to take a market risk, many businesses prefer to leave profits in an interest-earning commercial checking account known as NOW accounts (negotiable order of withdrawal). NOW accounts are available only to sole proprietorships and partnerships unless a corporation is not-for-profit. However, several other avenues might be explored.

- High grade commercial paper,
- Municipal bonds,
- Treasury bills or tax anticipation notes, and
- Certificate of deposit.

Check with the bank's investment advisor or a stock broker for the best plan for your business.

O. Uniform Commercial Code

Check and see what your State reference is to the Uniform Commercial Code it made vary from State to State

P. Securities Regulation

Many financing plans for small businesses involve, at least in part, the issuance of securities. Some of the most common forms of securities utilized by small businesses are common or preferred stock, limited partnership interests, debt with an option to convert into stock, and warrants to purchase stock. Debt financing obtained from parties other than commercial lenders also may involve a security.

Securities must be registered with the Secretary of State's office before being offered or sold unless the securities are exempt from the registration requirements. Persons selling securities also may have to be licensed by the Securities Department. If the business is seeking securities financing in any states, it will also have to comply with federal and other states' securities registration requirements. Consult an attorney about whether your financing plan involves securities and the applicable registration requirements and exemptions.

What are some of the ways that you may grow your business profits?

____
____
____
____

Q. Business Location

The location of the business often is determined by the type of business. Many sole proprietor operations are run in the home. Indeed, some occupations make that desirable and you are entitled to certain tax deductions which can be determined by discussing your business situations with an attorney or Accountant. You must check local ordinances regarding owning and operating a business from your home.

1. Can you operate your business from your home?

____
____
____
____

2. Are there tax benefits to operating a home business?

____
____
____
____

3. What professional can assist you in the setup of your home business?

____
____
____

R. Opening an Office

If the decision is made to have an office outside the home, a reputable real estate agent specializing in leasing or selling commercial space can help determine a quality location. Take as much time and care in choosing a business site as if choosing a home. The average employee spends 25% of his/her time at work and the environment should be as conducive to business as possible. In addition, a local office furniture and supply store can give valuable help in getting the office set up. It can assist with everything from color schemes to company logo design. Shared office space is another alternative whereby space is rented on a yearly, monthly, or even hourly basis. Conference rooms, office equipment, and mailing address use are but a few options.

Small Business Incubators are now operating throughout various states offering entrepreneurs extensive office facilities, shared clerical staff and equipment and technical business assistance.

1. How would you open a business outside of your home?

   ____
   ____
   ____
   ____

2. When should you use a real estate professional?

   ____
   ____
   ____
   ____

3. What are small business incubators?

   ____
   ____
   ____
   ____

4. Where would you like your business location?
____
____
____
____

5. Which community should your business be located?
____
____
____
____

6. Will your business be local, national, or international?
____
____
____
____

S. Temporary/Emergency Personnel

If your business had additional employees, chances are someone will be ill or unexpectedly absent for personal reasons. If this absence will create major inefficiencies, consider contacting a local employment agency. Temporary services can supply clerical personnel and, in some instances, workers for light industrial positions. A temporary replacement can usually be on the job within a few hours.

The company will charge an hourly rate based on job description. If dis-satisfied with the help provided, there generally is no charge. Check the yellow pages of the local telephone directory for Temporary Employment Agencies. A popular trend now is the hiring of virtual assistances to work on short term projects for your business.

If known in advance that an employee will be out of the office (*i.e.*, vacation, scheduled surgeries, paternity or maternity leave, etc.), contact your local college or university and ask for their placement offices. Students often stop by to check bulletin boards for local job offerings.

When should a business consider the hiring of a temp agency or a virtual assistance?

____

____

____

____

T. **Public Relations/Social Media**

Public relations can be simply defined as "doing good things and then making an effort to alert people that you have accomplished them." In a practical sense, it means getting the word of the positive, newsworthy things that happened in or at your place of business to the media so they, in turn will tell the story to their audiences your potential customers. When this happens successfully, the end result is publicity.

Good publicity is any news that is of potential interest to the people in the community. People make news. Employee promotions and awards make news. Events make news, business openings, special promotions, anniversary celebrations, participation in or sponsorship of a community activity. Innovations are news of a new product and/or a new service.

The more consumers read, see, and hear about business positive accomplishments, achievements, and activities, the greater the awareness will be of you and your business in the local community, resulting in a better image. Awareness and a good image are what can set a business apart from competitors.

A good public relations marketing tool is social media. Social media takes on many forms: internet forums, web blogs, social blogs, micro blogging, social networks, content communities, podcasts, application software, E-magazines, pictures, videos, rating (liking and disliking) and social book marking to name a few social media allows you to reach an unlimited number of potential customers at one time.

1. What is public relation?

____
____
____
____

2. Why is public relation important?

____
____
____
____
____
____
____

In some instances, "protection" may be sought for a product, service, new invention, or printed material. Following is a brief discussion of the three primary kinds of intellectual property protection: patents, trademarks, and copyrights.

U. Patents

A patent is a grant of a property right by the United States Government to the inventor (his or her heirs or assignees). The grant is made through the United States Patent and Trademark Office.

- Utility patents may be granted to anyone who invents or discover any new and useful process, matching, Article of Manufacture, or composition of matter, or any new and useful improvement thereof. Utility patents are granted for a term which begins with the date of the grant and usually ends 20 years from the date it was first applied for, subject to the payment appropriate maintenance fees.

- Design patents may be granted to anyone who invents a new, original, and ornamental design for an Article of Manufacture. Design patents last 14 years from the date the patent was granted. Currently depending on the size of the business, the cost ranges between, $190-$380 to file a design patent application. This fee is subject to change annually on October 1st per the federal fiscal year. No maintenance fees are required for design patents.
- Plant patents may be granted to anyone who invents or discover asexually reproduces any distinct and new variety of plant. Plant patents are granted for a term which begins with the date of the grant and usually ends 20 years from the initial patent application date.

Each patent application is a unique document that is prepared individually by the inventor with or without the help of a patent attorney. The first step in developing an application is a search to be sure the invention is indeed new, unique, non-obvious and for utility patents useful. When the document is prepared, it is filled with and examined by the United States patent and trademark office. All fees may be revised annually, taking effect October 1st the beginning of the federal government's fiscal year. Some patents can be costly. If you do not have the total amount to cover the cost, you can apply for a provisional patent which is in the range of $50-$100 until you can generate the funds to cover the invention. A provisional patent is good for 3 years. Many people seek an attorney or a business that specializes in assisting clients in obtaining patents that can result in substantial costs. You can contact your State's main library which may have a Department devoted to patent and staff to assist you in the application process. In Chicago, Illinois the Harold Washington Library has a Patent Department and helpful staff.

V. Federal Trademarks

Federal trademarks are obtained from the United States Patent and Trademark Office (USPTO), Federal trademark application filing fee range from $275-$375 per international class. You may file your trademark application online which provides a cost savings of $50 per application at the agency's website. You can also call the office and request the paper form.

W. State Trademarks

You may want to consider setting your business apart by registering for a state trademark through the Secretary of State. Any individual, firm, partnership, limited partnership, limited liability company, corporation, association, and union may do so. The mark must be used in your state before it may be registered and examples of this use must be submitted with the application for registration. Currently, the filing fee is $10.00 for the initial application. This is additional protection that your business name cannot be used by another entity.

If the trademark is used within one state only and thus does not qualify for federal registration, state registration is a good idea. State registration; however, does not offer the same level of protection provided by federal law.

The main benefit of state registration is that it notifies anyone who checks the state's list that the mark is owned by the registrant. This fact will lead most would-be users of the same trademark to choose another one rather than risk a legal dispute with the registered mark's owner.

If the mark is also federally registered, a would-be user of the same trademark is presumed to know the trademark is federally registered, and state registration is not necessary.

X. Copyrights

Copyrights protect the author, generally allowing him/her to control the copying of his/her work. The Library of Congress will provide registration once the appropriate form is processed, along with the required fee(s) and the copy(ies) designated for the type of work. Additional information, forms, and electronic filing can be done through the Library of Congress website www.copyright.gov.

In closing, you have been given information within these pages to assist you in making an inform decision as to whether starting a business is feasible to you. You can decide on a full time or part time while maintaining your 9-5. You can decide if you want to start up a business or acquire an established or franchise business. If you have an idea that is marketable then you can consider opening a business. A hobby, skill, or talent (*i.e.*, baking, sewing, etc.) can often be used to create a business venture that can be lucrative. Then you can decide if your business will be mobile, online, or a brick and mortar. The decision is all yours and no one can decide for you. You got options.

1. What is the difference between patent, trademark, and copyright?

   ____
   ____
   ____
   ____

2. List the item(s) that you need to patent for your business:

   ____
   ____
   ____
   ____

3. List the item(s) that you need to trademark for your business:

   ____
   ____
   ____

____

4. List the item(s) that you need to copyright for your business:
____
____
____
____

In addition, this booklet contains information for business startup; however, times and trends do change and you need to seek out those changes prior to business set up; and once you have an established business you must stay updated to the ever changing laws, as well as what is current and the best practices in your perspective industry.

Y. <u>References</u>

A few tips are shared from the below resources that you may contact for additional information:

State of Illinois Business Guide

Small Business Administration

Entrepreneur Magazine

Forbes Business Magazine

I. Creating A Business Plan

This Business Plan taken from www.Lawdepot.com (FREE BUSINESS PLAN) will assist you when creating a plan for your business. Be sure to indicate on the form that this document is confidential.

Start with the name of your business: ______________________

Business Address: ______________________________________

Business Phone Number: ________________________________

Date: ____

List the Management Team:

____

____

____

____

____

____

Below is a list of subjects, along with detailed information to help you create your business plan, and it may not apply to your business in its entirety:

Executive Summary
Vision/Mission Statement and Goals
- Vision Statement
- Goals and Objectives
- Keys to Success

Company Summary
- Company Background
- Resources, Facilities and Equipment
- Marketing Methods
- Management and Organization

Ownership Structure
Internal Analysis
Products and/or Services
Market Assessment
Examining the General Market
Customer Analysis
Industry Analysis
Strategic Alternatives
Strategic Implementation
Production
Resource Needs
Human
Financial
Physical
Sourcing/Procurement Strategy
Marketing Strategy
Hedging, forward pricing, options
Contracting
Insurance
Performance Standards
Financial Plan
Financial Projections
Contingency Plan

Provide the following information:
Business Name:
Business Address:
Business Phone no./Fax no.:
Business Email Address:
Business Website:
Date:
List the Key Players in the Business:

II. Executive Summary

This section is a summary of the information from the pages that follow. Prepare it last, after the business plan has been written. It should not exceed two pages. Headings to use in the Executive Summary:

A. Vision/Mission Statement
B. Company Summary
C. Products/Services
D. Market Assessment
E. Strategic Implementation
F. Expected Outcomes

III. Vision/Mission Statements, Goals and Keys

A. Vision/Mission Statements

The vision/mission statements are clear summaries of where the business is headed. It describes what the business produces, who products are produced for, and unique business characteristics. It will reflect the values of the management team and the type of business culture you are trying to create.

B. Goals and Objectives

What do you want your business to achieve? Be specific in terms of financial performance, resource commitments (time and money) and risk.
When will various milestones be achieved?

C. Keys to Success

What do you need, or must happen, for you to succeed?

IV. Company Summary

The material in this section is an introduction to the firm.

A. Company Background

What does your business do?
Who were the founders of the business?
What were the important milestones in the development of the business?

B. Resources, Facilities and Equipment

With what do you produce your products or services?
What are the land, equipment, human and financial resources?
Who provides them?
How are resource providers rewarded?

C. Marketing Methods

What is your annual sales volume in dollars and units?

Explain how you work with others to improve returns. This may include a strategic alliance with suppliers or customers that you can leverage.
Do you use forward contracting, options, or futures? If so, how?
How much does it cost to produce and deliver your products and services?
How is contracting used?

D. Management and Organization

Who is currently on the management team?
How have management responsibilities been divided among the management team?
What are the lines of authority?
Who acts as the president/CEO? spokesperson? Chief Financial Officer?
Who determines employees' salaries and conducts performance reviews?
What is the educational background of the management team members?
What is the management team's reputation in the community?
What special skills and abilities does the management team have?
What additional skills does the management team need?
Who are the key people and personnel that make your business run?
Who do you go to for advice and support?
Do management and employees have avenues for personal development?
Sketch a diagram of lines of authority for your operation.

E. Ownership Structure

Who are the primary stakeholders in your business?
Describe the legal form of your company, such as partnership, proprietorship, or corporation.
Do you need special permits to operate, or a record for inspections? If you do, please describe them.

F. Social Responsibility

What environmental practices do you follow?
What procedures do you use for handling chemicals?
What noise/dust/timing/odor policies do you have?
What will be the roles of management and employees in community organizations?
What will be your involvement at the local/state/national level in commodity organizations?
What training and new employee orientation practices will you offer to insure proper handling of hazardous materials and safe operation of equipment?

G. Internal Analysis

What are the strengths and weaknesses of your firm?
What are the relative strengths of each enterprise or business unit within the firm?
What are the core competencies (things you are doing better than others) of your firm?
What things can you build on? Think only about the things that you can control.
Suggested areas to consider:

- *knowledge and work*
- *financial position*
- *productivity*
- *family*
- *lifestyle*
- *location*
- *resources*

What enterprise or business unit shows promise?

V. Products and/or Services

Describe the products and services you plan to sell.
How is your product or service unique?
Are you producing a commodity or a differentiated product?
How does your product or service compare to other products in Quality? Price? Location?
What experience do you have with this product/service?

VI. Market Assessment

A. Examining the General Market

How is the market characterized?
Are there clear segments in the market? Describe them.
What important customer need(s) is the market not currently fulfilling?
What is the growth potential for each segment of the market?
What opportunities and threats does your firm face?
What does an analysis using the Five Forces model (for additional information google Five Forces model) suggest about your industry? Who is your competition (in light of the Five Forces)?
What trends, relevant to your business, do you see?
What are the drivers of change?

What political and legal issues do you face, such as zoning, environmental laws, inspections, etc.?

B. Customer Analysis

Who will be your customers?
What do you sell to each of the customers?
How does your product/service solve a key customer problem?
How difficult is it to retain a customer?
How much does it cost to support a customer?

C. Industry Analysis

Gather statics in your particular industry to develop the trends. What is the profit? Who are the leaders? What are the projections?

D. Strategic Alternatives

Research the problems in the industry and how you plan to get around it. Come up with a plan that your business will not experience those issues.

VII. Strategic Implementation

A. Production

How will you produce your product?
What value will you create and capture with your product?
What is your competitive advantage?
What technology will you use, (i.e., reduced tillage, GPS systems, etc.)?
What processes will you use to produce products?
What growth options will you use to develop the business unit?

- *Enterprise Expansion*
- *Replicate*
- *Integrate*
- *Network*

What is the anticipated timeline?

B. Resource Needs

In order to effectively organize your business, you need to insure the resources are available. Assess those needs here.

a) Human
What skills are needed?
How will human resources be acquired?

b) **Financial**
What level of financial resources will be needed?

c) **Physical**
What type, quantity and quality of physical resources will be required?

C. Sourcing/Procurement Strategy

On what do you base a decision to buy products or services? Price? Quality? Convenience? Extra service? A combination?
By what venue will you find suppliers — local dealer, Internet, direct from manufacturer, etc.?

D. Marketing Strategy

What is your sales plan?
What advertising and promotion will be used to increase sales/awareness?
Where will you sell products/services?
Will you use the open market or contracts?
Do you have a preferred market outlet?
Are you a qualified supplier for a specific processor or buyer?
How will you price the product?

a) **Hedging, forward pricing, options**
How will you use these to mitigate your risk?

b) **Contracting**
Will you use production or marketing contracting to reduce risk?

c) **Insurance**
How will you use crop, liability and other insurance?

E. Performance Standards

What performance standards will be used to monitor this enterprise or business unit?
What are acceptable performance standards?
What yield or output levels could you attain?
What efficiency levels will you reach?
What procedures will be used to monitor performance?
Who is responsible for monitoring performance?

What industry benchmarks will be used to assess performance?

VIII. Financial Plan

A. Financial Projections

How will you fund the business?
What is your desired debt and equity position?
Who will provide capital debt funds?
What role will leasing play in your financial strategy?
Will you use outside investors for equity capital?
How will you manage the financial risks your business faces?
What operating procedures, such as developing cash flow budgets or spending limits, will you have to ensure adequate money for debt repayment?
What are the important assumptions that underlie your projections? These assumptions may be associated with both external and internal factors.
What financial aspects of your business (equity, asset growth, ROA, ROE, etc.) will you monitor?
What procedures will be used for monitoring overall business performance?
What level of performance will your business shoot for? These should be targets for next year and in five years. They should be financial performance standards used to monitor the overall business.
What yield and output levels could you attain? What efficiency levels will you reach?

B. Contingency Plan

What will you do if you can't follow through with your primary plan?
How are you preparing for an emergency in your business?
How will the business function if something happens to one of the key members of the management team?

10 QUESTIONS TO ANSWER WHEN STARTING A BUSINESS

1. BUSINESS NAME
2. BUSINESS STRUCTURE
3. BUSINESS PLAN
4. BUSINESS ASSISTANCE AND TRAININGS
5. BUSINESS LOCATION
6. FINANCING BUSINESS
7. TAX IDENTIFICATION NUMBER
8. DUNN & BRADSTREET NUMBER
9. REGISTRATION FOR STATE AND LOCAL TAXES
10. BUSINESS LICENSES AND PERMITS

Dr. Eurydice Moore, Business Consultant

Founder of Eurydice

- Assisted Churches, Schools, and Agencies in acquiring over 3 Million in Resource Development Funding
- An Author of 4 books: Riddy Ann against the ODD, how to set up a Not-for-Profit, A-Z guide in for profit set up, Resource Development a New level of Dimension
- Grew up in Chicago's East-Garfield Community & graduated from Lucy Flower H.S.1974
- Graduated from Central YMCA in A.S degree in Medical Laboratory Technology 1976
- Graduated from College of St. Francis in B.S. degree in Health Arts 1984
- Graduated from Spertus in M.S. in Human Services Administration 1986
- Graduated from Concordia University in M.A. in Urban Education 1993
- Graduated from Northern Illinois's in Advance Certificate in Entrepreneurship Program 1991
- Graduated from Midwest Theological Institute in Indiana in Ph.D. Pastoral Counseling 2004
- Completed City of Chicago's Business Affairs & City College Business Start up 2007
- Completed Mormans Consulting Group's Business Coaching & Business Strategies Trainings 2016
- Medical Laboratory Technician at Rush, Cook County, Mount Sinai, Mary Thompson University of Illinois of Chicago Hospitals 1973-1985
- Educator & Work Study Coordinator at Lucy Flower H.S. 1985-1991
- Guidance Counselor at Morton Career Academy 1991-1995
- Over 30 years of combine Non-for-Profit experiences at Chicago Public School System, Churches, Social Services Center, Safe Haven Community Skill Center & Hannah Community Development Center 1985-2004
- Established Eurydice Moore & Associates 2004 to presence served over 12,000 clients in distribution of free grant and resource development information, incorporation, and 501(c)(3)
- Established Eurydice January 2016 to offer business set up, coaching,

trainings & development, incorporation, 501(c)(3) set up, grant writing, and resource development.

- Internet & Radio Personality 2005-2007
- CAN TV program in Non-Profit & For-Profit Business Resource 2007-2009

Author's Contact Information:

Dr. Eurydice Moore
eurydicemoore1@gmail

Discounted books are available to those who are interested in teaching from this booklet. You may contact me at the above-mentioned email address for discounted books, Consultation Services, Training and Development, and/or Speaking Engagements.

To add to your arsenal, PURCHASE MY BOOKs "Not-for-Profit Business" and "Resource Development".

OTHER BUSINESS RESOURCES

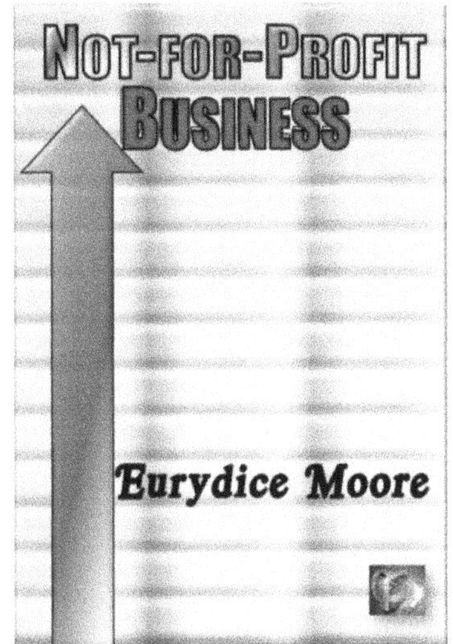

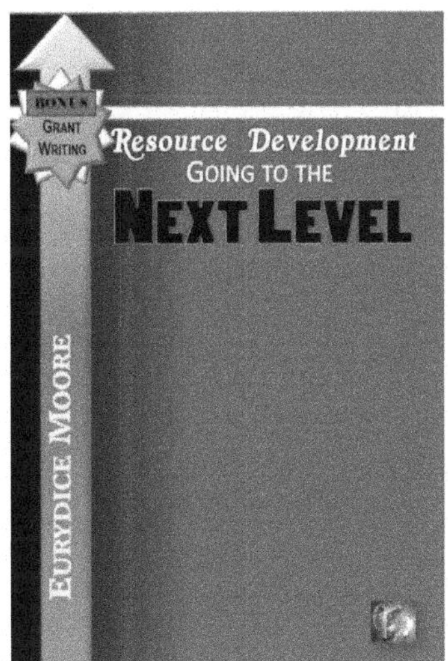

LIFE STORY OF THE AUTHOR THAT LED TO BUSINESS VENTURE

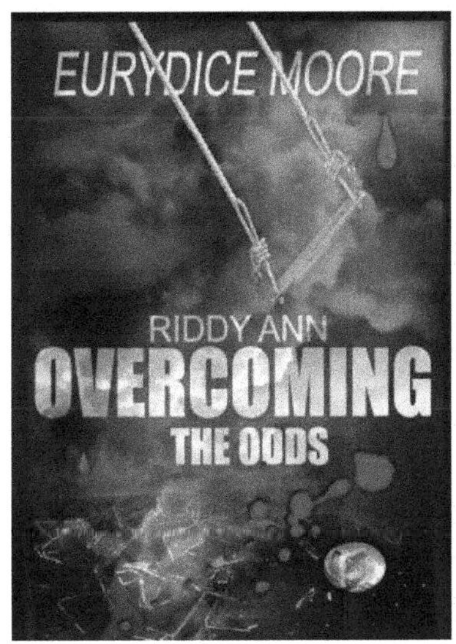

www.ingramcontent.com/pod-product-compliance
Ingram Content Group UK Ltd.
Pitfield, Milton Keynes, MK11 3LW, UK
UKHW051129260726
13967UKWH00010B/2946

9 780998 922324